KU-326-492

McGraw-Hill Education: *Leadership Essentials Series*

DHIRUBHAISM

THE REMARKABLE WORK PHILOSOPHY OF
Dhirubhai Ambani

Other titles by AG Krishnamurthy:

The Invisible CEO
ISBN: 0070597626
Price: INR 250

Desi Dream Merchants
ISBN: 0070608229
Price: INR 215

Other titles in Leadership Essentials Series:

80/20 CEO—Vaman Kamath
Shrinivas Pandit
ISBN: 0070617546
Price: INR 99

Quality Leader—Venu Srinivasan
Shrinivas Pandit
ISBN: 0070620881
Price: INR 99

Nurturing Leader—Prathap Reddy
Shrinivas Pandit
ISBN: 0070617554
Price: INR 95

Strategic Thinker—Mallika Srinivasan
Shrinivas Pandit
ISBN: 0070617538
Price: INR 99

McGraw-Hill Education: *Leadership Essentials Series*

DHIRUBHAISM

THE REMARKABLE WORK PHILOSOPHY OF

Dhirubhai Ambani

Foreword by

Mukesh Ambani

From the author of 'The Invisible CEO'

A G KRISHNAMURTHY

Tata McGraw-Hill Publishing Company Limited

NEW DELHI

McGraw-Hill Offices

New Delhi New York St Louis San Francisco Auckland Bogotá Caracas
Kuala Lumpur Lisbon London Madrid Mexico City Milan Montreal
San Juan Santiago Singapore Sydney Tokyo Toronto

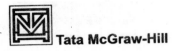 **Tata McGraw-Hill**

Published by Tata McGraw-Hill Publishing Company Limited,
7 West Patel Nagar, New Delhi 110 008

Copyright © 2007, by A G Krishnamurthy

Sixth reprint 2007
RYDZCRYYRDYDA

No part of this publication may be reproduced or distributed in any form or by any means, electronic, mechanical, photocopying, recording, or otherwise or stored in a database or retrieval system without the prior written permission of the publishers. The program listings (if any) may be entered, stored and executed in a computer system, but they may not be reproduced for publication.

This edition can be exported from India only by the publishers,
Tata McGraw-Hill Publishing Company Limited.

ISBN-13: 978-0-07-063373-5
ISBN-10: 0-07-063373-8

Head—Professional and Healthcare: *Roystan La'Porte*
Publishing Manager: *R. Chandra Sekhar*
Editorial Executive: *Sauvik Mukherjee*
Senior Copy Editor: *Sandhya Iyer*

Asst General Manager—Production: *B.L.Dogra*
Junior Manager, Production: *Sohan Gaur*

Information contained in this work has been obtained by Tata McGraw-Hill, from sources believed to be reliable. However, neither Tata McGraw-Hill nor its authors guarantee the accuracy or completeness of any information published herein, and neither Tata McGraw-Hill nor its authors shall be responsible for any errors, omissions, or damages arising out of use of this information. This work is published with the understanding that Tata McGraw-Hill and its authors are supplying information but are not attempting to render engineering or other professional services. If such services are required, the assistance of an appropriate professional should be sought.

Typeset in Tej Composers, WZ-391, Madipur, New Delhi 110 063, and printed at
Pashupati Printers Pvt. Ltd., Delhi 110 095

To

admirers of **Dhirubhai Ambani**

all over the world

'We bet on people'.

- Dhirubhai Ambani

Reviews on *Dhirubhaism*

"…An easy read: you can finish it in about 90 minutes flat! But its influence will stay for a long time—in some cases, for a lifetime…"

The Economic Times

"In this 96 page slim volume, Krishnamurthy, in a very crisp and simple format and doing away with all management-speak and business jargons, pinpoints about 15 Dhirubhaisms…"

The Indian Express

"A new 'ism' in the making?"

DNA Money

"The Red book of Dhirubhai Ambani…"

The Hindu

"It is a collection of memories of a person, who created brands like *Vimal* and *Rasna*…"

The Times of India

"…Provides a simple yet accurate look at the modern day corporate culture and solutions to everyday office situations…"

www.timesgroup.com

CONTENTS

FOREWORD

More than ambition, challenging adversity provided my father, Dhirubhai Ambani, with the adrenalin that spurred him to build a fine business enterprise in less than three decades. An obstacle, he liked to say, is an opportunity, not an obstruction. It compels you to find ways to duck it, circumvent it and vault over it. A set-back is no more than an interlude to prepare for a leap forward. Hard times must indeed beckon you to strive harder to excel in your endeavours.

The roots of such derring-do can be traced to his origins. My grandfather was a school teacher. *Papa* had little formal education. The world was his university and the rough and tumble of life itself served as his tutor. He started from scratch without access to finance or to the network of the influential and the powerful. Today the manifold ventures of Reliance bear tangible witness to the business acumen he developed during this stern apprenticeship.

But to some of us – his immediate family members and colleagues and friends of long years – the intangible aspects of his legacy are far more precious. Time and again I have been asked: what drove Dhirubhai to scale the summits of entrepreneurship? I could cite many factors though one of them I think counts for more than all others.

Throughout his adult life, my father nursed dreams about the grandeur of his country and the wellbeing of its people.

He had pride in being an Indian and, therefore, the impatience to see that his country must be equal to others. Even in the face of trying odds, he never wavered in his resolve to contribute to India's emergence as a strong, prosperous and caring nation, at peace with itself and with the world. His faith in the Indian people was equally steadfast. It was rooted in their intellectual, cultural and spiritual accomplishments over many millennia. These led him to believe that given a congenial environment they would yet astonish humankind with their feats in every field of creative activity. In this respect, Dhirubhai was first and foremost a thorough Indian patriot in thought and action.

From his days as a young petrol attendant in Aden, he never ceased to explore unorthodox ways and means which would allow India and Indians to re-discover their self-worth. Early on he reckoned that the only way forward lay in simultaneously pursuing three goals: quality education, empowerment of individuals and communities; and the inculcation of the spirit of enterprise in the state and society alike. Progress on these fronts, he argued, must go hand-in-hand with the development of social and physical infrastructure required to modernize the economy and make governance more transparent and accountable.

In India, such thinking was deemed to be heretical when Dhirubhai began to stride the corporate stage. This was an era of licences and quotas which caged entrepreneurship. But that did not dampen his ardour. He put to use the latest technological innovations and the most advanced management practices for the speedy expansion of his enterprise, which grew into an empire. In the bargain, he rattled pedigreed corporate houses, earned the ire of sections of the political class and the bureaucracy and attracted scorn and invective from powerful segments of the media.

What galled Dhirubhai's critics and detractors was his success in outwitting them at every turn. Not only did he dream bigger and bigger dreams but he also found novel methods to realize them. One such way was to ensure that ordinary citizens shared in the wealth he created. To the under-privileged and the un-empowered he showed by example how they could fulfil their hopes for a brighter tomorrow for themselves and for their children.

No one doubts any more that such a vision brought about a paradigm shift in the history of Indian business. It helped to evolve a mass consciousness about the promise of entrepreneurship to enrich people in their hundreds of thousands and to propel India into the league of advanced nations. The radical nature of the vision became even more evident when the Indian economy began to undergo reforms and exposed itself to the draughts of globalisation.

With added vigour he urged his compatriots to abandon self-doubt, erase the word 'impossible' from their lexicon and keep hope alive in the midst of grave uncertainty. He called on them to cherish not the idea of power but the power of ideas. No one, he insisted, can claim a monopoly over them.

His own ideas questioned conventional thinking, accepted dogma and intellectual sloth. And he did this armed with native intelligence and earthy wisdom.

The intent behind such questioning was to unlock the potential contained not only in every drop of petrol but in people as well. In his view they were gifted with more talent and determination than they were prepared to admit. He therefore steered them to realize their potential in full measure. Such mentoring gave many, including myself, their corporate baptism.

For Dhirubhai, Reliance meant something more than a mere business venture. Its collective capacity had to be harnessed to fulfil loftier ambitions. It is this credo that guides my own efforts to turn Reliance into a global brand of an enabled and enabling India. Indeed, our ventures like Reliance Retail aim to empower the humblest farmer and the village woman without a voice of her own. To what end? The answer is clear: to firmly link our businesses with our core belief that what is good for India cannot but be good for Reliance.

As Dhirubhai did in the course of his life-time, we too strive to dream big, powerful dreams. We draw inspiration from his passionate eagerness to take risks to ensure the success of our businesses. We seek to meet the standards he laid down to attain success: every rupee we invest must fetch better returns than every rupee that others invest in the same field. Every business plan must be executed in less time than anywhere else in the world. Levels of productivity must be second to none.

Let me inject a personal note here. I learnt from *Papa* that you have to be demanding to get colleagues to perform at the highest possible levels. But you also need to be compassionate towards them in personal matters. Indeed, he believed in the power of corporate altruism to transform the lives of the helpless and the vulnerable.

This book narrates how *Papa* spotted petrochemicals' potential in its infancy to establish Reliance and swiftly turn it into a super brand. He invented Vimal which just as swiftly became an aspirational icon. He transformed investment in Reliance into a project for prosperity for millions. In the process he gained unique access to the common man and woman of India. They shared his vision; they reposed their trust in him; they also showered him with affection.

In the last years of his life, his most acerbic critics too acknowledged the scale of his achievements. The praise did please him hugely though it did not surprise him. He had taught us that even malevolent criticism mattered more than the flattery of sycophants. The teaching echoed a dictum from the Upanishads: 'truth lies everywhere and, partially, even in error.' He thus regarded critics as potential comrades and adversaries as potential allies much as he regarded the poor and the meek as his potential partners.

The only way that we can pay homage to his memory is to continue to draw lessons from the life he led, from the values he cherished and from the dreams he dreamt. In many ways his journey from a village in Gujarat to the commanding heights of the corporate world serves as a metaphor for a resurgent India. History has summoned my generation of entrepreneurs to act as the avant-garde of this resurgence. That summons—I can almost hear *Papa* pronouncing it— is what sustains our confidence, feeds our hopes and allows us—shareholders and employees of Reliance—to walk ten feet tall today.

MUKESH D AMBANI
Chairman
Reliance Industries Ltd.

PREFACE

Anyone who has ever met Dhirubhai remembers their first meeting with him, vividly. It's difficult not to—he was such an incredible life-force. I remember my first meeting with him like it was yesterday, and mostly, because it was quite an eventful one.

The year was 1975 and Vimal Sarees had just begun making waves. The advertising for it was sporadic and was handled by a small shop, but Vimal's nylon sarees were creating quite a buzz with housewives who were recommending them highly, as nylon was the rage at the time. At that time, I was an Account Executive working with Shilpi Advertising and like all eager ad executives we too at Shilpi began making cold calls to Reliance for their business. We met various officials both in Ahmedabad and Bombay, but didn't get the opportunity to meet Dhirubhai. One fine day, when we called his office we were given an appointment to meet him at 11:30 a.m, at Reliance Textile Industries Private Limited, as the company was known then, at Court House, Dhobhi Talao, Bombay.

Dutifully, Shilpi's Chief Executive, Creative Chief, Branch Head and I were at the appointed hour. We waited for the meeting to commence. And waited...And waited... Minutes ticked by as did the hours. Two of my colleagues shook their heads disapprovingly and left stating that it was the strangest thing that had ever happened to them. Finally at 6:30 pm, the Chief Executive and I were summoned. By this time, we were really exhausted and tired to the bone and all that we wanted to do was to wrap the meeting up as quickly as possible and head back.

Dhirubhai started talking. Suddenly, the room was charged with a kind of buzz that was hypnotic. Though not a good elocutionist, when he spoke, you listened with rapt attention, because of the passion with which he expressed himself. He had the ability to carry you along with him and it was very difficult to tear your mind away. There we sat, the two of us listening mesmerized to his dreams and plans for Vimal, as our fatigue slipped away. We did not get the account. But after a few weeks Dhirubhai asked me to join him. And the rest is history.

Unlike other bosses, Dhirubhai respected and appreciated frankness and openness from his employees, a great deal. It takes a big man to do that—not everyone likes a frank employee! I remember a time when during my early days at Reliance, I was told by a few colleagues that Dhirubhai was unhappy with my work. Naturally this feedback upset me quite a bit, but instead of internalizing it and feeling hurt, I decided to ask Dhirubhai about it. I am grateful to this day that I did, simply because of what he told me during that meeting. He looked me straight in the eye and informed me that there was no truth in what I was told. And more importantly he added something that I will never forget: 'If I want to say something to you, *I will tell you.*'

That set the tone of our relationship. He knew that if something upset me he could depend on me to be open and frank about it, and I on my part always knew that he would be equally open and honest with me. And so began an eventful relationship that spanned for over 28 years.

There was another incident that I remember vividly which made a deep impact on me and was probably the reason why the creative department at Mudra was mortally terrified of stray errors! I was in Bangalore on a business trip when I got a call from Dhirubhai. He was driving to Reliance Patalganga and had stopped his journey to get me on line. He told me there was a mistake on one of our advertising billboards that he had driven past and would I rectify it immediately? I flew back on the next flight and got it done. But that was the intensity of his eye for detail. And my first exposure to it. Even if he was whizzing past a billboard his sharp eye could pick out a mistake and his impatience would want it rectified on the spot! I on my part vowed that that would be the last time that I gave him an occasion to do so.

Even though he was a perfectionist and an impatient one at that, he was an extremely informal boss. It might be difficult to believe this, but I've never made an appointment for a meeting with him however big and important he became. Anytime I wanted to meet him, all I had to do was to knock on his door and walk in, regardless with whom he was meeting. I would walk around his desk to where he was seated and he would handle the issue then and there—if it was really important he took me aside for a couple of minutes. The only details I've had to plan were to check with his secretaries if he was in town and that he was not in any sensitive meeting with his visitors. He had this open-door policy for most of his people. He knew he could trust us not to waste his time and he definitely didn't want us to waste ours, waiting to meet him!

Dhirubhai was a university all by himself and with every interaction with him one came away always learning something new. This book is a collection of all the lessons that I've learned working with him and my observations on his unique people handling skills. Dhirubhai began Reliance Naroda with a very small team. He built a formidable empire in a blisteringly short span of time—just three decades—but more importantly he built a strong team of leaders. He did it all with no degrees in management or psychology. But yet he mobilized ordinary men into performing extraordinary feats.

He was truly a one in a million human being and I was extremely blessed to have had him as my boss. He taught me many things that have transformed an ordinary executive that I was, to be the Founder, and CMD (Chairman and Managing Director) of Mudra, an advertising agency that grew from nothing to one of India's largest. I would have never achieved it without him. It would be a shame if I let his extraordinary teachings gather dust. Which is why, I have decided to continue sharing what I've learned from him with any one who is interested to be like him.

There is one person to whom I'm extremely grateful for his invaluable contribution towards this book—Shri Mukesh D. Ambani, Chairman, Reliance Industries Limited. I thank him for so magnanimously finding the time despite his hectic schedule to write the foreword for this book. It has been a great privilege and honour for me to have known him over the past two and a half decades and work with him for the last four years. It was his encouragement and quiet support that helped me nurture the concept of *Dhirubhaism* to fruition.

I would also like to thank three remarkable people who I consider my gurus:

- Giraben Sarabhai—for refining my aesthetic sensibilities and inculcating in me the ability to distinguish the beautiful from the mundane.

- Dhirubhai Ambani—for teaching me the art of handling life like a winner and dealing with the successes and failures that come with it.

- Dr. Verghese Kurien—for showing me that even from an insignificant town like Anand it is possible to make India the largest milk producing nation in the world—all that is required is to believe.. in India.

A person is considered to be blessed if they have one good guru in their lives. I guess I must be phenomenally lucky to have been given three of India's best!

In addition, I thank:

- My colleague Minnie Abraham who has made it possible for my columns *AGKspeak* in *Business Standard*, my books—*The Invisible CEO, Desi Dream Merchants* and the present one, *Dhirubhaism* to become reality.

- T N Ninan and the *Business Standard* for their continued support of *AGKspeak*, the platform that helped launch *Dhirubhaism*.

I hope this little book will act as a guide or a manual for the thousands who deeply admire Dhirubhai and are eager to know more about his remarkable work philosophy. I'm sure even if a couple of Dhirubhaisms are incorporated and faithfully adhered to in our lives, we'll start witnessing a remarkable change. Success is a definite outcome. So here's wishing you all the best and God Bless.

A G Krishnamurthy

ABOUT DHIRUBHAI AMBANI

Born on 28 December, 1932, Dhirubhai was the fifth child of Hirachandbhai and Jamnaben Ambani. He left his hometown Chorwad, Gujarat for Aden, at the age of 17, to work at A.Besse & Co. Nine years later he returned to India and set up Reliance Commercial Corporation, a trading venture. He moved from trading in spices to yarn and in 1966 began textile manufacturing at Naroda, Gujarat. He then began manufacturing up the value chain—textiles, then yarn, polyester and petrochemicals, then ventured into oil and gas refining and subsequently oil exploration building a multi billion dollar corporation in the process. Dhirubhai financed his plans by going to the capital markets in 1977. He convinced a new breed of investor—the middle class community—to put their faith in what was then a little known textile company. His subsequent phenomenal performance and rewarding of their trust created an entirely new investing culture in the country.

Within a span of just 25 years, he created the country's largest Fortune 500 corporation. The Reliance Group is a living testament to his indomitable will, and his unrelenting commitment to achieving his goals. The Group's track record of consistent growth is unparalleled in Indian industry. Today its turnover represents nearly three per cent of the Indian GDP.

The corporate philosophy Dhirubhai followed was simple: Think big. Think differently. Think fast. Think ahead. Aim for the best. He ingrained this philosophy into the team he nurtured and ensured that they continuously set their sights on higher goals.

He remained the same Dhirubhai all through his life—his personal tastes remained simple, his friendships endured the journey, his generosity shone undiminished, and his quest for excellence remained unshaken. All through his sixty-nine years—as a child in Chorwad, an employee in Aden, as a spice and yarn trader in Bombay and as the Chairman of India's largest private sector corporation—he consistently displayed remarkable leadership traits.

The *Bhagvad Gita* states, 'The actions of a great man are an inspiration for others. Whatever he does becomes a standard for others to follow.' Dhirubhai's life exemplified this.

DHIRUBHAISM

There is a new *ism* that I've been meaning to add to the vast world of words for quite a while now. Because, without exaggeration, it's a word for which no synonym can do full justice— '*Dhirubhaism*'. Inspired by the truly phenomenal Dhirubhai H Ambani it will denote a characteristic, tendency or syndrome as demonstrated by its inspirer. Dhirubhai on his part, had he been around, would have laughed heartily and declared, "Small men like me don't inspire big words!" That for instance, is a classic Dhirubhaism—the tendency to disregard one's own invaluable contribution to society as significant! I'm sure everyone who knew Dhirubhai well will have his or her own little anecdote that illustrates his unique personality. He was a person whose heart and head both worked at peak efficiency levels, all the time. Extraordinary vision coupled with phenomenal compassion—this was his remarkable work philosophy, and that which I would like to define as 'Dhirubhaism'.

DHIRUBHAISM

DHIRUBHAISM *1*

Roll up your sleeves and help.
You and your team share the same DNA

During Vimal's heady days, sometime in the late seventies, Reliance had organized a fashion show at the Convention Hall, Ashoka Hotel, New Delhi. As usual, every seat in the hall was taken, and there were an equal number of impatient guests outside, waiting to be seated. Those were the nascent days of India's fashion industry and Vimal's fashion shows were hugely popular.

Stories abound about how people would try by hook or crook to get a pass for these events. One of the main reasons why Vimal's shows were so popular was because they were audio-visual extravaganzas. We, the creators and organizers of these events were constantly pushing the envelope as far as the medium was concerned and we would make sure that every show had something truly spectacular for the spectators to look forward to. Our efforts were richly rewarded with each show running to full capacity in all the towns to which we took these road shows.

That evening in Delhi was no exception and we were close to being mobbed that day by guests both real and suspect! I was of course, completely besieged, trying to handle the confusion, chaos and protests when to my amazement and I must confess immense relief, I spotted Dhirubhai at the door trying to pacify the guests! Even while I was trying to come to terms with this unique sight, the first thought that crossed my mind was a deep sense of admiration. Let me explain why I was so impressed.

Dhirubhai was already quite a name to reckon with and a VIP at the time. He had caught the attention of the nation and he was beginning to be treated like a celebrity wherever he went. He was the at helm of a company that was well on its way to becoming an empire. The Reliance Textile Mill at Naroda had just been declared by the World Bank as 'India's finest textile mill by developed country's standards' and it was around this time too, that Dhirubhai created history in the Indian stock market by throwing open the shares of his company to the average Indian middle class investor, thus beginning a whole new trend. India was just getting her first glimpse of his prodigious genius.

To put it simply, he had become a 'big shot'.

Yet at the Convention Hall that day, a stranger would not

have been able to identify him as one. In a flash Dhirubhai had transformed into one of us—just another member of Reliance's team of managers. Rather than driving up at the last moment in a gleaming limo and then imperiously summoning and questioning the people in charge about the chaos, he slipped in unannounced, sized up the situation in the blink of an eye, quietly rolled up his sleeves and proceeded to help. He could see for himself that all of us were neck-deep in trying to get the situation under control. Most bosses in his place would have given the manager a piece of their minds. Not Dhirubhai.

When things went wrong, he was our best ally. He was the first person to sense that the circumstances would have been beyond our control, rather than it being a slip on our part. He trusted the capabilities of his core team, implicitly. His first instinct was to always join his men in putting out the fire rather crucifying them for it. It was this deep trust in his men that served as the glue that held us fast to him.

Because it is hard to walk out on or let down a person who places such a high degree of faith in your efficiency and capability. He believed in our abilities in very much the same way a parent does, in his own child. It was his faith in us that gave us strength and inspired ordinary men to achieve extraordinary feats.

Sounds too good a boss to be true, doesn't he? But then, that was Dhirubhai.

I believe that the success of Reliance cannot be attributed to the qualities and achievements of one individual, or even a group of individuals, but has to be viewed as a triumph of a process, and a spirit that binds the entire Reliance family together.

– Dhirubhai Ambani

DHIRUBHAISM 2

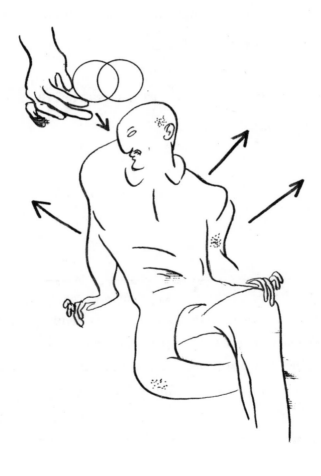

Be a safety net for your team
and they will perform wonders

When we began Mudra in 1980, we were a completely atypical advertising agency. To begin with we were not headquartered in India's advertising capital—Mumbai (Bombay). Secondly, we had acquired a roster of Indian entrepreneurs as our clients who found in us the 'Indian professional agency' that they were desperately seeking. Both these aspects worked in our favour and in an unbelievable nine years' time we grew to be among the top three agencies in the country. It was an achievement that was the first of its kind on the advertising scenario.

None of the big players had grown so big, so fast. To all of us in Mudra it was just one of those targets that we had set for ourselves and once we got there we paid little attention to it as we were so preoccupied with the road ahead. Little did we realize that our entry into the 'big league' was not looked upon kindly by some members of the industry.

It was at this time when the rumours began. Like all rumour mills do, these snide remarks and insinuations started being churned out gradually. My business ethics were brought into question through petty talk and party gossip. There were many stories, but the ones that found its way into the press implied that we at Mudra had offered discounts to our clients which was the reason we had grown so big, so quickly! I tried to ignore them because they were so clearly untrue, but the very injustice of these accusations slowly began to affect me. During those days, I would regularly

come to Mumbai to meet with Dhirubhai. In fact, I would
board the Gujarat Mail in Ahmedabad every Sunday night,
and return on Wednesday morning and I did this for the
first six years without a single break! Whenever we met
we would discuss everything pertaining to the agency—
the work, plans for Mudra's future etc. I had many
opportunities to pour my heart out to him about this wave
of viciousness that was threatening to engulf me and Mudra.
But never once during any of these interactions did I bring
up the topic. I guess I did not do it because I was trying
very hard to put up a brave front!

Many meetings came and went. Dhirubhai, on his part was
fully aware of what was going on, even though I did not
realize it then. Since I did not bring up the topic, neither did
he. Until one day, during a particularly nasty spell, he looked
at me with the utmost compassion and gently asked me if I
needed any help in combating it. When I saw the look on

his face I was overwhelmed. I had never received so much empathy from any employer before. This was all that I needed—his assurance that I was not alone in this battle.

I quickly brushed his question aside and replied that I could cope. But when I left his room, I left feeling ten times taller. I felt I could take on an entire army of naysayers!

And I did. I offered to throw open Mudra's books to an impartial audit recommended by the Advertising Agencies Association of India (AAAI) provided all the other agencies followed suit. Almost magically the rumours and false reports quieted down.

That was the outcome of just knowing that Dhirubhai was on my side. Knowing that he would fight my battles for me if I ever needed him to, knowing that he was there to support, encourage and believe in me, unquestioningly, regardless of the outcome. He was our safety net who gave us the courage to fly.

When you are confident that there is someone out there to break your fall, there is no limit to how high you will fly. It is always the fear of falling that inhibits a person from making a daring leap.

Reliance's success is a reflection of India's capabilities, the talent of her people and the potential of her entrepreneurs, engineers, managers and workers.

— Dhirubhai Ambani

DHIRUBHAISM *3*

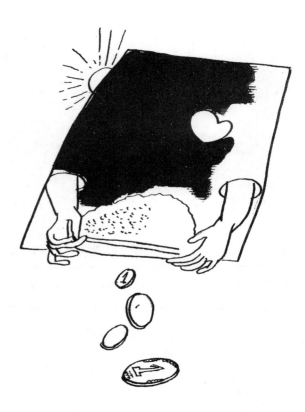

Be a silent benefactor

Philanthropy is one of the ways large and sometimes medium sized industrial houses contribute to society. It's a nice way of saying 'Thank you' and 'We care' to a society that helped them grow. The dictionary defines philanthropy thus: 1.The effort or inclination to increase the well-being of humankind, as by charitable aid or donations 2. Love of humankind in general. 3.Something, such as an activity or institution, intended to promote human welfare. Dhirubhai was widely known and acclaimed as a great and visionary industrialist but philanthropy was not a trait publicly associated with him. In this section, I will tell you why.

There are many people in this world who make a donation and make sure that the entire world hears about it.

Dhirubhai was not one of them.

And then there are those who lend a much-needed helping hand to a relative or a friend in need, and then make sure that the rest of his relatives and friends hear about it.

Dhirubhai was not one of them.

Then there are those who view large donations as a valuable public relations tool that benefits not only the needy but is also tremendously useful to garner goodwill for their company.

Dhirubhai was definitely not one of them.

On the other hand, he was a philanthropist of the most unusual kind. When he gave, and that was nearly all of the time, he made sure that no one talked about it.

I can quite confidently say that he was the only silent

benefactor whom I've ever come across. That is why Dhirubhai's name does not spring easily into the minds of many, when they talk about great philanthropists. Why exactly he was so keen that his acts of generosity went unadvertised no one will ever know. But I can only surmise that his innate graciousness and nobility forbade him from doing so.

To those of us who knew him well, his open-handed generosity, his ability to sense our need and come to our rescue even before we had the courage to articulate it to him, makes him the most generous philanthropist of them all.

During the seventies and even as recent as the eighties, extra money was always hard to come by. There were no credit cards, no friendly banks pestering us to take up their loan offers—in fact getting a loan from a bank was almost impossible for the common man. But yet our needs were the same as it is today— family ties, help with a vehicle purchase, weddings, medical emergencies and so on. And most us had no one to turn to. No rich uncle or older brother with generous coffers. All that we had as a fall-back option were our savings and our salaries. But for those of us who knew Dhirubhai, money was never a concern. He wouldn't let it be. Almost all of us have received of his generosity and sometimes when he knew the severity of the situation, he would gift away sizeable amounts!

Like the time he helped out an acquaintance who was indebted to him and couldn't repay the money because he had a drinking problem. Instead of writing him off, Dhirubhai doubled the loan so that he could recover from his losses, straighten himself out when he realized the gravity of his plight and become self-sufficient to repay the entire amount. Which he did!

It was not always money that he helped people with. He would help a struggling friend with whatever he required to get him back on track. It could be time taken off to pen a letter cheering him up in a foreign land, it could be a job for the son of a schoolmate, it could be sending an air ticket, new clothes and an airport pick up for an old family gardener to enjoy the sights of Bombay, it could be flying an entire makeshift hospital to help a village back on its feet after a devastating earthquake, it could be sending across truckloads of vegetables to far away flood hit places. All these acts of kindness were quietly, silently and efficiently executed. No pomp and ceremony preceded or followed these gestures. In fact, most of his beneficiaries were not even aware that their Good Samaritan was Dhirubhai.

But when a hand was stretched out in need, an acute longing struggled for articulation, it never went unnoticed by this man whose generosity was not limited to doling out cash, but extended to a far greater temperament; that of spirit, heart and mind and can only be defined as limitless.

I live the Gita.

– *Dhirubhai Ambani*

DHIRUBHAISM *4*

Dream big but dream with your eyes open

This might sound a bit paradoxical but believe it or not, this is how Dhirubhai not only dreamed unbelievably big, but was able to see these 'impossible' dreams of his come true in his own lifetime. Not many people get to do that! On the one hand, he was a dreamer and a most audacious one at that. On the other, he made sure his 'eyes were open' all the time, as he put it! What he meant was that even when he dreamt, his path forward was clear to him. He was very clear about his competencies and he dreamed his dreams within that framework. His goal might have seemed distant and unattainable to the onlooker, but Dhirubhai was very clear about the path that would take him there. The mountain peak is not visible to a climber standing at the foothills because it is beyond his view; but he still makes his way to the top.

When Dhirubhai was only a sales person at Shell's trading outpost in Aden he dreamt that he wanted to set up his own refinery one day! As dreams go, it was as preposterous as it could get. But that was what made Dhirubhai different from most other dreamers. He knew even then, that the only 'impossible' aspect about his goal was the world's opinion of his ability to achieve it. It was not what *he* believed and knew of himself.

His phenomenal achievements have showed India that limitations were only in the mind. And that nothing was truly unattainable for those who dreamed big. Whenever I used to try and point out to him that a task seemed too big to be accomplished he would brush it away with the reply: "No is no answer!" Not only did *he* dream big, he taught all of us to do so too. His one-line brief to me when we began Mudra was: "Make Vimal's advertising the benchmark for fashion advertising in the country." To understand what an apparently improbable demand it was, you must realize that in the early eighties, we were just a tiny, fledgling agency, tucked away in Ahmedabad, struggling to put a team in place! High fashion was as distant to us, as the moon from the earth! But Dhirubhai never viewed a situation for what it was currently, his eye was ever focused on what it could grow to become and he would work hard to make it achieve its full potential.

When we presented the seemingly insurmountable to him, his favourite response would always be: "It's difficult but not impossible!" And he was right. We, in that tiny little agency called Mudra did go on to achieve the impossible. In a record nine years' time we became one of the top three agencies in the country, besides being the largest Indian advertising agency, as the other two were multinationals. Vimal's fashion shows meanwhile, were again unprecedented in the country, both in its size and scope. Grand showroom openings, stunning experiments in print, poster and television work all combined to give the brand a truly iconic image. As an agency too, we broke fresh ground in many areas. And thus, Dhirubhai's belief in our potential came true. But way back in 1980, no one would have believed it could have ever been possible. Except Dhirubhai.

But though he dreamed big, he was clearly able to distinguish between perception and reality and his favourite phrase 'dream with your eyes open' underlined this. He never let preset norms govern his vision yet he worked night and day familiarizing himself with every little nitty-gritty that constituted his dreams constantly sifting the wheat from the chaff. He was the hardest worker I've ever met. At any given time, he was more familiar with the ins and outs of a project than most of us were.

Even though he ventured into areas he had no prior experience in, he was pretty confident of his ability to learn. This was how, as he put it, even though he dreamed, none of his dreams turned into nightmares. This was what gave him the courage to move from one orbit to the next despite tremendous odds. This was how he, a boy from Chorwad, Gujarat became the creator of India's largest private sector company.

A vision has to be within reach not in the air.
It has to be achievable.

— Dhirubhai Ambani

DHIRUBHAISM 5

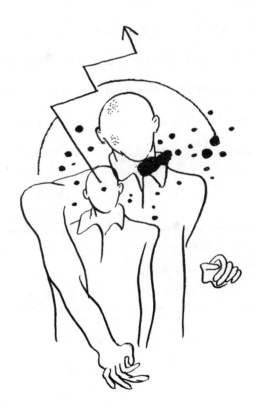

The arm-around-the-shoulder leader

There are some leaders who are fearful of getting too close to their subordinates. A certain 'royal' distance is always maintained to shield them from over familiarity with their colleagues.

Dhirubhai, however was totally unafraid of getting close to his men. Physical proximity came naturally to him. He would, without a second's hesitation slip his arm around our shoulders and walk a few metres if he wanted to discuss anything with us. I have never seen any CEO of any big organisation do this (why, *I* never adopted this myself!). It was Dhirubhai's very own signature style. Whenever I went to meet him, and if on that day, all the time that he could spare me was a short walk up to his car, he would instantly put his arm around me and proceed to discuss the issues at hand as we walked. With that one simple gesture, he managed to achieve many things. I was put at ease instantaneously. I was made to feel like an equal who was loved and important enough to be considered close to him.

His cheerful *'Kya dost'* was the way he greeted everybody. Regardless of class, creed or religion. And that was truly how he felt. Perhaps the reason why he could, so effortlessly draw us close to him. Although in the beginning an introvert would tend to feel a bit awkward with this proximity, within seconds all his barriers tended to fall away.

To put it simply, when you put your arm around someone, communication becomes effortless. Misunderstandings and hidden resentments bubble up to the surface quicker and it became easier for Dhirubhai to sort out even the tiniest glitches developing in a relationship, before it snowballed into unmanageable proportions.

This was perhaps why he was so effective as a leader. He had mastered the art of communication. I don't think at any time, any of us could have complained that there were any misunderstandings between him and us. The credit for that goes entirely to him. He treated his colleagues as precious assets and he would work very hard in ensuring that the communication lines between us and him were always open.

Even years later, when he had very little time on his hands for a casual chat, we could at any time ask to meet him and he would ensure that he made time for us. Just like the short walk we had from his office to his car. It might have only been a ten minute encounter, but I would walk away from this 'arm-around-the-shoulder' meeting feeling so good about myself and the work I was doing!

This tendency that he had, to draw people towards him, manifested itself in countless ways. Putting his arm around us was just one of them. Dhirubhai would never, ever exude an air of aloofness and exclusivity. He was always inviting people into sharing their thoughts and ideas, rather than shutting them out. On hindsight I think it must have required a phenomenal generosity of spirit to be that inclusive. Most people are slightly apprehensive about inviting too many opinions that could be contrary to their point of view. But Dhirubhai went out of his way to get people to open up. If he learnt that there was value in their point of view he would instantly embrace it, discarding his own without any feelings of remorse! I have often thought that it takes a very brave man to have such an open mind.

Yes, this was one of the things that was uniquely Dhirubhai
—that warm arm around my shoulder that did much more
than words could in letting me know that I belonged, that
I had his trust and more significantly, that I had him on my
side!

---

*We must learn to trust. For several centuries,
Indians have been brainwashed to distrust other
Indians. This saps national energy.
Distrust kills initiative. Distrust compels people to
maneuver and manipulate. Trust and transparency
stimulates entrepreneurship.*

– Dhirubhai Ambani

DHIRUBHAISM *6*

The Dhirubhai theory:
Supply creates demand

Dhirubhai was not an MBA. Nor was he an economist. In fact he was only a Matriculate. But yet he took traditional market theory and stood it on its head. And succeeded. Yes, at a time when everyone in India would tentatively build capacities only after a careful study of market expectations, he went full steam ahead and created mammoth manufacturing plants with unbelievable capacities for the times (way back in 1980, initial capacity of Reliance Patalganga was 10,000 tonnes of Polyester Filament Yarn (PFY) while the entire market for it in India was approximately 6000 tonnes). This was where he baffled the rest of his peers. It was very difficult for them to come to terms with the fact that the vision of someone like Dhirubhai who did not have the right academic pedigree, could possibly be right.

But Dhirubhai's lack of education in economic theory was more than compensated by his tremendous capacity to learn. And his most uncommon common sense. He had very sharp instincts too, which were no doubt backed by years of reading, studying market trends, careful listening and his own honed capacity to forecast, but yet despite all this preparation, one can't deny that it required undeniable guts to pioneer such a revolutionary move. Courage of conviction was another thing that Dhirubhai had in abundance. Once he was confident about his homework, he would venture out boldly into completely unknown terrain with nothing short of, than the daring of an explorer. It was his firm belief that expanding the market would benefit not just Reliance but the entire industry and eventually the country. All that he needed was his experience with his textile mill at Naroda that taught him the important co-relation between size and sales. His unusual theory of providing supply to create demand was the outcome of his ability to make intelligent deductions from his own experiences.

The consequence was that the market blossomed to absorb supply and the consumer benefited when the prices came crashing down. The more of a product that was available, the more affordable it became. It was just plain, simple logic. But to make this logic work, Dhirubhai also knew that he needed speed and efficiency. He was constantly and swifty upgrading technology, coming up with innovative schemes to raise money from the markets, ploughing it back into his plants and increasing capacities, all at the same time. The result was plain for all to see. When an industry is in demand, the players naturally increase, and our economic landscape changes for the better. The Patalganga plant for instance was in no time humming at maximum capacity and as a result of the plant's economies of scale, Dhirubhai's conversion cost of the yarn in 1994 came down to 18 cents per pound, as compared to Western Europe's 34 cents, North America's 29 cents and the Far East's 23 cents. In no time Reliance was exporting the yarn back to their technical collaborators, DuPont, USA!

A more recent example where this theory has shown phenomenal results has been with Mukesh Ambani taking this vision forward with Reliance Infocomm[1]. In the timeline of India's mobile telephony there will always be a very clear 'before Reliance Infocomm and after Reliance Infocomm' segmentation. The numbers say it all. In January

[1]Now Reliance Communications

2003, the mobile subscriber base was 13 million. About 16 months later shortly after Reliance IndiaMobile was launched, it had reached 30 million. And by the end of July 2006, it has touched 111.23 million[2] with prices of handsets and talktime getting more and affordable by the day.

Yes, this was yet another unusual skill of Dhirubhai's—his uncanny knack of knowing exactly how the market is going to behave.

Think big, think fast, and think ahead.
Ideas are no one's monopoly.

– Dhirubhai Ambani

---

[2]TRAI Press Release, 10 August, 2006

DHIRUBHAISM *7*

Money is not a product by itself.

It is a by-product, so don't chase it

Might seem like strange words from someone who was India's richest industrialist! But this was the belief by which Dhirubhai lived his life and what he taught me. For instance, when he briefed me about setting up Mudra, his instruction was clear: 'Produce the best textile advertising in the country', he said. It was all the instruction that he gave me.

This was Mudra's mandate. He did not breathe a word about profits—not a single word about wanting Mudra to become the biggest or the richest ad agency in the country. Instead, great advertising was the goal that he set for me.

It was in Dhirubhai's nature not to state the obvious. Especially when he was teaching us something. He would only show us the way and leave us to learn our lessons on our own. His message in the instruction that he gave me was implicit. When you do good work, it is bound to bring recognition. As the saying goes: A lit candle can't be hid. When your work is recognised, as the sales people say, it 'Gets your foot in the door'. In other words, prospective clients and customers will listen to what you have to say and some might even come up to you and offer you their business because they are impressed with your work. More work, in turn means more money. So simply put, money is the by-product of good work.

A by-product is something that you don't set out to produce. It is not your primary motive. It doesn't govern your choices. A by-product is the spin off when you create something larger. For instance, when you turn logs into lumber, sawdust is your by-product and a pretty lucrative one it can be too! Most people mistakenly assume that people become billionaires by single-mindedly pursuing the accumulation of wealth. They couldn't be further from the truth!

You might wonder, what could be so wrong about focusing on money rather than focusing on creating a good product? The answer is simple. When money becomes your prime motive you tend to cut corners, because your priority is about how much you can save or how much money you can make. When quality is compromised, the result will be a bad product. You might be able to fool some of your clients for some of the time, but before you know it, word will spread within your business community about the inefficacy or unreliabilty of your product.

Haven't you seen it happen so often? Not only will your bad product scare away all *your* clients and customers, it will actually drive them to your competitors! When this happens, you realize that you've signed your own death warrant, businesswise.

But on the other hand, a good product is like your personal ambassador who will forge long-lasting relationships with your clients. Not only will you have a steady roster of good business partners, they will invariably recommend you to their circle of acquaintances. That, is the secret of creating an unending supply of money.

Money, is the value of your product. It is not and can never be a product on its own. Except maybe for the Reserve Bank of India who regularly print it by the sheets, for us!

If you work with determination and with perfection, success will follow.

– Dhirubhai Ambani

DHIRUBHAISM *8*

Leave the professional alone

This quality was as rare a trait in the seventies and eighties, as it is today. Despite all their fervent protestations and much as people would like to believe, owners, managers, clients and the rest don't leave the professional alone. They are very quick to hire their services, and in fact even go to great pains to select the best in the industry and compensate them handsomely.

But once in their employ, a strange thing happens. The professional who has been hired solely for his highly reputed expertise is suddenly treated as an extension of the owner/manager's persona! He then proceeds to become a mere tool whose job is to execute the owner/manager's bidding.

Every time I come across this, which is much too often, I am reminded of Dhirubhai, and how his management techniques used to be and still remains so refreshingly different. For instance, way back in the late seventies when we decided to open an agency of our own, he handed me my first task which was—the naming of the agency. I carried a short list of three names to him, two westernized and one Indian. It was a very different world back then, when every thing Anglicized was considered 'in' and 'upmarket'. There were hardly any advertising agencies with Indian names barring my own ex-agency Shilpi and a few others like Ulka and Sistas. And since the ad world was heavily influenced by the west, it was only understandable that everyone chose the same path for easier acceptance among clients and within the peer group.

Dhirubhai looked at my list and asked me what my choice was. I said 'Mudra', the only Indian name on it. He asked me why it was my preference and I explained that it was the only name that suited my personality. And the spirit that I had planned for the agency that I was to head. I was very Indian, both in my outlook and my mannerisms and an Anglicized name on my visiting card would make me seem pretentious and contrived. He listened and said "Ok, go ahead and do it!" That was it. No further questions were asked. No suggestions offered, no words of advice. Just a plain and simple go ahead.

That was just the beginning. He continued to give me total freedom in all my decisions thereafter. There was absolutely no supervision and no policing of me or my executives! His utter trust in me was what pushed me to ensure that I never, ever let him down. He treated me like the professional

he had hired for the job and I strove to fulfill my side of the

bargain.

Mudra's initial years which were during the eighties,

coincided with Reliance's growth from a textile

manufacturing unit to a company well on its way to being

the empire that it is today. Dhirubhai would constantly be

pressurized to send across various people to me as part of

his business obligations. However, he would never force

me to hire anyone, however highly he was recommended.

All that Dhirubhai would do, would be to attach a little

note on the person's resumé which read "On Merit" . The

rest was up to me. It were little gestures like these that let

me know that he believed in my professionalism and more

importantly he trusted that I would do the right thing.

I guess the simplest strategies are often the hardest to adopt.

This was the secret of Dhirubhai's legendary management techniques. They were not out of a book. They were a skillful blend of head and heart. A unique method that mined extraordinary performances from ordinary executives.

Give (your people) the youth a proper environment.
Motivate them. Extend them the support they need.
Each one of them has infinite source of energy.

They will deliver.

– Dhirubhai Ambani

DHIRUBHAISM 9

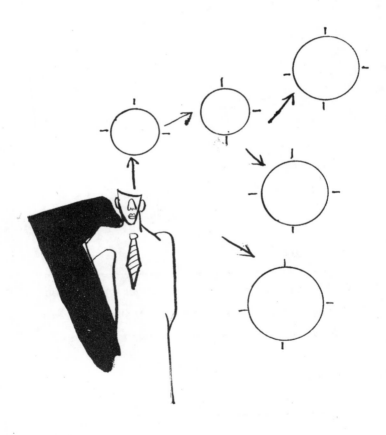

Change your orbit, constantly

To understand this statement, let me explain Dhirubhai's 'orbit theory'. He would often explain that we are all born into a previously decided orbit. It is then up to us to push our way out of it and progress to the next. A kind of evolution, so to speak, to the next level. We could of course, choose to live and die in the orbit that we are born in, like so many people do.

But that would be a criminal waste of potential. In truth, it
is a kind of primal instinct in all of us to want to evolve to
the next stage just like our ancestors did. There could be
many reasons to this, a desire to survive in changing
environments being the primary one. We are all familiar
with the consequences of failing to evolve—we would
become extinct, like dinosaurs. A few people like Dhirubhai
understand this very early in life and fuel forward faster
than others, enjoying the rewards that prime movers do!
Coming back to Dhirubhai's orbit theory, when we push
ourselves into the next orbit, we benefit not only ourselves
but every one connected with us as well. It takes each and
every one of us to constantly do this if we need our country
to progress from a 'developing nation' to a *developed*
one. There used to be a time when our country's growth
rate was just 4% and was sarcastically referred to as the
Hindu growth rate! Look at us today. We are galloping

along at a nice and healthy 7% to 8%. This is no miracle. It is the product of a handful of determined orbit changers like Dhirubhai, all of whose efforts have benefited a larger sphere in their respective fields.

In a small way, I too have experienced the thrill of changing orbits with Mudra. Way back in the eighties, we shot up from a being a small agency in Ahmedabad to become the country's third largest national agency, in just under ten years. When we achieved this, I realized that it opened up a whole new world of possibilities and opportunities not only for us but for a lot of youngsters joining the profession as well. Bigness brings with it certain indisputable advantages: When you are bigger, you are able to buy better. This means you don't have to compromise and settle for the less affordable in the market place. Better buying power also gives you the ability to invest better. A good investment always rewards you in the future.

You also get to innovate and experiment. We all know that
true growth can only happen with a certain degree of risk
taking and experimentation. Bigness affords you the ability
to encourage experiments. This is how we were able to
branch into path-breaking innovations like MICA (Mudra
Institute of Communications, Ahmedabad) which must be
one of its kind in the world.

You can set industry benchmarks when you are big. Taking
on a leadership role is a natural consequence of size and
as a leader you can influence the industry in which you
operate!

However, there is one thing to bear in mind. When you
change orbits as you grow, your passage from one to
another is bound to create a lot of friction. There used to
be a time when, the more successful Dhirubhai was

promising to become, the more vitriolic his detractors became. As he so rightly pointed out once: 'My success is my greatest enemy'. In one of his AGM addresses, he remarked: "Our critics obviously do not feel happy when we perform well. Now that we are forced to take some giant steps in the immediate future, such attacks are only natural. ...When you pass through an orbit, it creates friction. And that is natural."

Just as a space craft is engineered to break out of earth's gravitational pull, you too should be mentally strong to break away from forces that pull you back. And pull you back they definitely will. To take the same analogy forward, also make sure you develop a heat shield to protect you from vaporizing into thin air! Since friction is a natural consequence of breaking out of orbits, it's easy to get burnt badly if you don't have one. Friction makes its presence felt by rumours, lies, isolation, ridiculous assumptions that mirror the accuser's jealousies and even cleverly worded 'first hand reports'! Worrying about such strong negativity will only burn you up. Remember that if and when you do emerge unscathed, the joy of having succeeded is unparalleled and is the best amnesiac in the world. The good news is that your enemies from your previous orbit will never be able to reach you in your new one. By the time resentment builds up in your new orbit, you should move up to the next level. And so on, till you get stronger and bigger.

Growth has no limit at Reliance. I keep revising my vision. Only when you dream it you can do it.

– Dhirubhai Ambani

DHIRUBHAISM *10*

Optimism, the core of Dhirubhaism

If there was one person who can be credited with having taught the Indian middle-class to dream, it must be Dhirubhai. In the otherwise futile middle and lower middle-class world of the late seventies and early eighties, all tied up with endless red-tape and continual frustration, he blew in like a breath of fresh air, showing and proving to people that if he can make the impossible happen, so can they!

It all began in 1977—when a business- unfriendly banking system refused to loan him money for the upgradation/ expansion of his textile mill at Reliance Naroda. Dhirubhai was no stranger to borrowing. 'Profit will be yours, loss is mine' was his favourite catch-phrase as he borrowed from various small-time lenders to fund his trade ventures while he was in Aden and during his early Bombay years. He borrowed on such generous terms that people would come up and offer money to him! But Reliance Naroda required much more than small funds—it needed a couple of crores! So in a path-breaking move, he decided to throw open his company to millions of middle-class shareholders. No amount or no investor was too small for him. He took their money and their trust, performed phenomenally and in turn rewarded his 'bankers' as he called his shareholders, handsomely over the years. There are many who built their homes, married off their daughters and educated their children by selling off Reliance shares. At a time when it was impossible for the common man to get a loan from the bank for expenses such as these!

This was perhaps when the first seeds of the Optimistic Indian of today were sown.

Apart from Dhirubhai giving the middle-class the opportunity to dream, his own life-story served and continues to serve as a beacon of hope to many. He shared the same childhood as millions of other little village children of the pre-Independence era. Any one who has run around barefoot as a child because his parents could not afford to buy him footwear, walked to school, owned only two sets of clothes, would find a kindred spirit in Dhirubhai! But with a unique combination of determination, extreme hard work and an unbeatable optimism in his own abilities to make his dreams come true, Dhirubhai rose from his middle-class beginnings to create an empire that is not only India's No.1 private sector company but is also the first Indian private sector company to appear on the Fortune 500 list. Dhirubhai was extremely proud of his roots and would make it a point to bring it up in any conversation that lauded his success. Because as he put it, his life was the best proof that lineage and a privileged background were *not* mandatory requirements for success.

'Hope is your most powerful weapon' he pointed out, in his acceptance speech as The Dean's Medal was awarded to him by the Wharton School of Pennsylvania. Even when he was accepting this high honour, he was reaching out and infusing optimism in the minds of the average Indian middle-class person. That was the most wonderful quality of Dhirubhai. He never patted himself on the back, but used every award and recognition he was given to illustrate to the many out there that success was within reach if you tried hard enough. 'If one Dhirubhai can do so much, just think what a thousand Dhirubhais can do for this country.

There are easily a thousand Dhirubhais, if not more. I firmly and sincerely believe in this' he said. His words have not gone unheeded. He is the benchmark for many entrepreneurs today. He brought the phrase 'Think big' into the business world's lexicon. Indians today are making international acquisitions with the courage to make big strides. We as a nation are rapidly shedding our image as 'safe players'. Everybody today has a 'big plan'. Talk to a roadside vendor and you can see a restaurant in his dreams, talk to a driver and you can see a fleet owner emerging. Thinking big is everywhere and it's catching on even as I write this. Hope, has finally come to stay.

And we all have one person to thank for that— Dhirubhai.

He was, and will continue to be optimism's best ambassador.

Pursue your goals even in the face of difficulties, and convert adversities into opportunities.

– Dhirubhai Ambani

DHIRUBHAISM *11*

You can find a friend
in every human being

From the peon to the President, Dhirubhai had a friend in them all! This has got to be one of the most endearing Dhirubhaisms that I've seen. He could strike up a conversation with almost anybody regardless of their caste, class or creed. The best part was that *he* would do the listening most of the time.

He would break the ice initially and get them talking and then listen intently to everything they had to share, his hyper active mind learning all the time! He would constantly ask his driver, his peon, the paanwallah et al, how they handled their money and often kept their dreams and aspirations well in focus when he charted out a product plan or entered a new venture. It was his directive when Reliance Infocomm was at the blueprint stage, that a mobile phone call should be made cheaper than a post-card. At the time, in early 2000, the average cost of a mobile phone call was around Rs.16 and the price of a post card, Rs.0.50! Economies of scale aside, he knew exactly what the common man wanted. That was because he had many friends amongst them as well!

He was equally at ease with the heads of countries, corporations and powerful achievers alike. Again, he would listen intently to their views and opinions as well, learning where he could and helping them out whenever they needed it.

I guess he was every man's friend because he was genuinely interested in people. External trappings like money and power or the lack of it, did not cloud his judgment. Perhaps this is why he could, with perfect ease throw his arm around our shoulders and have an impromptu tête-à-tête anywhere. Power normally distances people from the common touch but it was definitely not so in Dhirubhai's case.

One of the more public instances when this was obvious was during the Economic Times Awards. Dhirubhai was honoured with a Lifetime Achievement Award and immediately after a standing ovation to the announcement, there was a crowd of press photographers all clamoring for his picture. A totally predictable and normal situation you might say. But what was markedly different about this one was that they were all trying to get his attention by unanimously calling out to him: 'Dhirubhai, Dhirubhai'. They did not address him as 'Sir', nor 'Mr. Ambani' as one would have expected them to, at such an august gathering. He was just 'Dhirubhai' to them, as he was to the Prime Minister and the President. And he smiled genially at all of them asking them to be patient and that he would give every one of them the shot they wanted! It was obvious they enjoyed a special freedom with him than they did with the other achievers on stage. Editors, journalists, press photographers…Dhirubhai had friends up and down the entire hierarchy.

He was '*Aapna* (our) Dhirubhai' to everyone who knew him. It was that wonderful sense of approachability that made him so beloved by all, despite his formidable power and stature.

I have trusted people and
they have put their trust in me.

– Dhirubhai Ambani

DHIRUBHAISM *12*

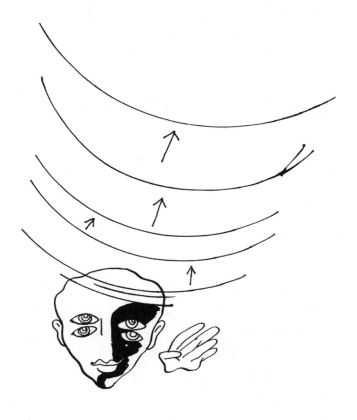

Think big

Whenever Dhirubhai had an announcement to make or a product to launch he would make sure that he would do it with spectacular style. Invariably it was on a scale unprecedented in the country. So much so that he set a precedent for fabulously dramatic and imaginative announcements.

As his advertising manager I have worked with him closely on some of these projects and I can assure you the impact that he created on his audience has them awe-struck and spell bound even to this day!

In the seventies when fashion shows remained by and large between the pages of foreign magazines, Dhirubhai and Reliance would organize mammoth events or road shows across the country for Vimal fabric. Those were the days of the Audio-Visual (AV) presentation and a two projector AV was considered an impressive presentation. The Vimal shows on the other hand had six projector presentations, accompanied by 40,000 watts of mind numbing sound and models walking on three ramps simultaneously! As you can well imagine the impact of so much beauty, visual effects and heart stopping music on a captive audience was nothing short of mind-blowing. Is it any wonder that crowds invariably charged into Vimal's shows paying scant heed to passes and seating restrictions!

Then came the eighties and the decade of the exclusive Vimal showrooms. Dhirubhai opened 101 outlets on one single day. It took an entire full page centre spread advertisement in newspapers to accommodate all 101 names. It was and still remains an unprecedented act. So impressive was this gesture that it is talked about with awe even today. Only Dhirubhai could have managed to swing a deal with a hundred plus retailers in one sweep.

If this was not impressive enough, when he opened the showroom at Bangalore, he had a helicopter showering rose petals and pamphlets onto an open-mouthed city, nearly all of whom had gathered to watch this amazing spectacle. Their minds already numbed with the phenomenon of Vimal, they were then led into 6000 sq.feet of glittering showroom space. Again, the impact was so tremendous it echoes even today.

Then came the Reliance Cup that began on October 8, 1987.

It was the first time the Cricket World Cup was brought into the country and for a nation of die-hard cricket fans, Dhirubhai and Reliance were instantly elevated to God-like status, even if it might sound a trifle exaggerated. It was a major event for the eighties and no private company had sponsored anything on that scale before. Needless to say Reliance will always be looked on as the prime mover of cricket in the country.

Even as Dhirubhai was periodically bombarding the nation with all these extravaganzas, he was simultaneously building his brand Vimal with an advertising budget never heard of before. We had an annual budget of Rs.3 crores in 1977 when the entire advertising budget for textile advertising in the country totaled all of Rs.10 crores and the average textile brand's annual advertising budget was no more than Rs.40 to Rs.50 lakhs! Visually stunning television commercials, extravagant splashes of colour in the daily press, double spreads in magazines probably the first of its kind, riveting posters in shops all combined to give the buyer a 360° visual feast which too, like all of Dhirubhai's other ventures continues to resound in the minds of people many, many years later.

It was his steady and consistent focus on the spectacular that contributed immensely to the brand image that Reliance carries even today. It is true that Dhirubhai and Reliance have now become synonymous with the fabulous and the spectacular, but they were not arbitrary gimmicks for publicity. The marketing and advertising blitzkrieg of the seventies and eighties laid the crucial foundation for the gigantic empire that the company is today. Dhirubhai proved that it pays to be big and spectacular!

For those who dare to dream, there is a whole world to win...Dream and dare.

– Dhirubhai Ambani

DHIRUBHAISM *13*

Hold on to your dreams...

H old on to your dreams and they are bound to come true. If there is one person who was living proof of this belief, it was Dhirubhai Ambani. Today, the world knows him as a highly acclaimed achiever and creator of India's spectacular world-scale plants. Most people must be aware that he came from an ordinary middle-class family. Just a matriculate, he set sail to Aden where he worked with A.Besse and Co, who was a distributor for Shell.

It was while he was selling lubricants and oil samples to the ships docked in Aden harbour that he first had a glimpse of what he really wanted to do—build a refinery of his own one day. He was only in his early twenties then. At long last, in 1995 when he was sixty three years old he performed the *bhumi puja* for Reliance Jamnagar, the world's largest greenfield grassroots refinery—his dream. It is undeniable that Dhirubhai was a man of exceptional calibre, and possessed uncanny vision but more importantly he had phenomenal determination to never let go of his dream. The temptations to do so I'm sure were enormous. He had his own lack of technical education to deal with, his lack of finances, his lack of safety nets.. the list was endless. But he found his way around every single one of the handicaps that he was faced with. He focused on his strengths—his willingness to learn, his capacity for enormous hard work, his quickness to pick up market information, his ability to respond with lightning speed and forged his way ahead. All one has to do is check the archives of any leading newspaper and you can see for yourself that his detractors and naysayers were plentiful. Every step he took was accompanied by a loud chorus of doubts, rumours and allegations, but gradually as they watched him successfully complete stage after stage in his building of Reliance, the negative reports grudgingly turned into words of praise.

Watching him as he moved ahead, his eye fixed on his goal served as tremendous inspiration to all of us who worked closely with him and also fired in us a determination to hold on to the dreams that we had for ourselves.

I can, in all fairness say that when we began Mudra, all that we had was Rs.35,000 and a dream. Our initial goal was to produce the best textile advertising in the country. In 1980, sitting at my desk in a small office in Ahmedabad which was miles away from Mumbai the advertising capital of the country, it really was quite an impossible dream. But persistence paid off and we not only produced iconic advertising, we grew to become one of the top three agencies in the country in a record time of nine years.

With this experience behind me, I can see how Dhirubhai was able to make his impossible dream come true. When you want something so badly, the Universe, as Paul Coelho puts it, nudges you in the right direction and conspires to make it come true. Your yearning gives you a certain sense of clarity that helps you see beyond obstacles and arms you with the knowledge that these roadblocks are only temporary. Often people give up on their dreams only because they are unable to see beyond the here and now.

But to get the Universe on your side, you will have to hold on fast to your dream even though you encounter many people, very often in the guise of well-wishers, and many situations that will try and take your dream away from you.

Hold on fast, know your strengths and you can make the most impossible dream of yours come true.

Don't give up, courage is my conviction.

– Dhirubhai Ambani

DHIRUBHAISM *14*

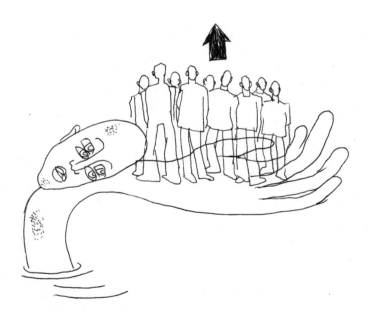

Bet on your people

As I mentioned earlier, I met Dhirubhai in 1975. A year later I took up his offer and joined as Advertising Manager for Reliance Textile Industries as it was known in those days. Within four years time, he gave me some seed money and asked me to begin an advertising agency all on my own! That was Dhirubhai.

That was the way he bet on us, his people. He took a four year old (in most other companies, I would have still been treated as a 'junior') and put me in charge of his money and a brand new company! Not only did he put me in charge, he *trusted* me completely. When I use the word 'completely' it is not an exaggeration. It is a fact. The only mandate he gave me was to 'produce the best possible textile advertising'. He set no financial targets, nor did he police me, or demand daily reports. As I would often tell my team at Mudra, he handed me the lock, and the key to a treasure.

In fact it was his philosophy of betting on his people that lay the foundations for the gigantic empire that Reliance is today. When he began Reliance Naroda, all that he had with him was a small team who possessed little technical know how. But Dhirubhai's ability to hand over complete charge to the people he picked for the job paid him back a hundredfold. The reasoning is simple: when some one places their entire trust in you to handle a job, you will try everything in your power and beyond, to assure him that he made the right decision by putting you in charge.

There were many times that the responsibility felt tremendous when he handed it to us. But his reply; 'No is no answer' would make us think again, his belief that we were more than capable to handle the job would fuel us with the determination we needed to complete it.

Admittedly, Dhirubhai was a shrewd judge of character and calibre. He could see skills in us we never knew we had. But his perceptiveness was only one half of his winning formula. It was his *courage* to bet on his people that was the other crucial component.

I realised what an important role courage played when, as Chairman of Mudra I decided to adopt this philosophy. The stakes are tremendous when you do so. For instance, when we decided it was time to take our creative work on Vimal to the next level, we did not approach the tried and tested superstars of the advertising world. We went to relative newcomers who showed promise and gave them the freedom to experiment. It is a daunting task to take the money of your most valuable client and entrust it to a hitherto untried talent. But the passion and the joy that they invest in your work is unparalleled and I have never regretted any of the bets that I have taken. Clearly not all my bets have paid off. But the rewards of the ones that did far outweighed the losses.

This philosophy of Dhirubhai's was very similar to all of his other beliefs. It was a simple viewpoint. It took tremendous courage. And it had spectacular results.

We bet on people.

– Dhirubhai Ambani

DHIRUBHAISM *15*

Be positive

The more you know about Dhirubhai's life, the more you will be surprised to know the enormity of the odds that he faced in the process of building Reliance.

Yet he never complained. We all knew about the endless licenses, the red tape and the bureaucracy that he had to wade through to get one project going.

Yet we never heard him grumble. Not once did he complain

about the country's lack of infrastructure or the lack of

systems and processes, or hostile business environments.

Not once did we hear him threaten to take his business

abroad. It was almost as if he accepted the inadequacies

of the day as a given and tried not to let what was missing

stop him from getting what he wanted!

'I consider myself a pathfinder. I have been excavating the

jungle and making the road for others to walk. I like to be

the first in everything I do' he reflected in one of his

speeches. I guess he was a pioneer at heart and maybe it

was this adventurous spirit of his that gave him the

wherewithal to take inadequacies in his stride.

When he required funding for the expansion of his mill and

the banks turned him down, he didn't waste time grumbling

about their lack of vision. Instead, he quietly found a way

out for himself. He went to the masses. It was a road that

would eventually change the landscape of the Indian stock

market and reward millions.

In the eighties when he needed licenses for the first of his backward integration projects at Patalganga, the license raj was in full reign. Apart from this the Planning Commission had made it mandatory for permission to be sought for material, capital, human resources, all decisions regarding production, increasing or decreasing capacity, etc. But yet Dhirubhai did not let the needless tediousness of setting up projects stop him from dreaming big. He dealt with all the red tape in his usual matter-of-fact manner and turned his focus on his business.

His positive attitude was so rewarding that not only did it benefit him, he helped rewrite the economic future of the country.

It would have been so easy for him to join the rest of the brigade, aim low and blame it on circumstance. Instead he did the opposite, he went ahead and built world scale capacity plants-like the 10,000 tpa polyester filament yarn (PFY) plant at Patalganga when the market in the entire country was only 6000 tpa! It didn't end there. He continued to build plants with enormous capacities setting his sights clearly on the world market.

Dhirubhai's story is a classic illustration of the power of a positive attitude. Reliance today stands as its towering proof.

'My advice to young entrepreneurs is not to accept defeat in the face of odds, and challenge negative forces with hope, self-confidence and conviction.
I believe that ambition and initiative will ultimately triumph. The success of the young entrepreneur will be the key to India's transformation in the new millennium.'

— Dhirubhai Ambani

AFTERWORD

Dhirubhaism found its beginnings on Feb 3, 2006 in a fortnightly column that I write for the *Business Standard*. Judging by the response that it received, it looked like Dhirubhai continues to be fresh and alive in people's memory. The least I could do was to share more anecdotes of what I learned from Dhirubhai with a generation who seemed to be thirsting to know more. Clearly, they were not satisfied with the couple of Dhirubhaisms that I had talked about— almost instinctively they seemed to sense that there ought to be more.

A few of my readers even went so far as to suggest publishing an entire book of Dhirubhaisms! This was the trigger that I was waiting for. They had articulated an idea that I have been nurturing for a while now. A kind of a handbook so to speak, of how Dhirubhai handled various issues and difficult situations. It is something that I myself resort to quite often. Whenever I am caught in a bind, I try and imagine what Dhirubhai would have done in my place, how he would have handled it. I've discovered it's a very effective technique to try and think like Dhirubhai! Doing so has helped me get around quite a few obstacles. His people skills were truly remarkable and his ability to overcome problems is now the stuff of legends. Besides, I have yet to come across a leader who could get people who were polar opposites to work together as a team.

This book takes the reader only about an hour and a half to read. But if at the end of this it can show you that all that it takes to achieve big is to adhere to simple philosophies like Dhirubhai did, then I would in some small measure, be echoing Dhirubhai's sentiment when he said: 'If one Dhirubhai can do so much, just think what a thousand Dhirubhai's can do for this country. There are easily a thousand Dhirubhais, if not more. I firmly and sincerely believe in this'.

His philosophy was breathtakingly simple and very fundamental—like his ability to trust. Or rather, his *courage* to trust. It might sound simple enough, but not many of us can do it. When Dhirubhai said: 'We bet on people', he followed it. They were not idle words. He actually took great risks with his team. That takes a lot of courage. But his trust was so complete and so uncomplicated that it was the very simplicity of his belief that rewarded him phenomenally. If we can follow just three or four of his life's mantras we will start witnessing a dramatic change in our lives, immediately.

The best tribute we can pay this truly extraordinary man is to work towards becoming a Dhirubhai ourselves, to discover the Dhirubhai within all of us.